The Light Betrayed Me

SANDOVAL

PAGE PUBLISHING
Conneaut Lake, PA

First originally published by Page Publishing 2024

ISBN 979-8-89315-121-3 (pbk)
ISBN 979-8-89315-169-5 (hc)
ISBN 979-8-89315-138-1 (digital)

Printed in the United States of America

Contents

Restoration

My light has dimmed
I hold on by a ray
Happiness was endless
Love so pure
A serene soul
Shattered by shadows
Tested faith
Peace an illusion
Hope diminishing
My light
Will you shine so bright again
Chase the shadows into the darkness
Restore faith
Give hope
Bring peace
My light
My love
My faith
My peace
Don't forsake me

I'm Tired

I'm tired of beating the odds
I'm tired of the trial and tribulations
I'm tired of being told that everything
  happens for a reason
I'm tired of defending myself
I'm tired of working so hard at something not to succeed
I'm tired I've been fighting since I was three
I'm tired, I'm done, I don't have any fight in me
I'm tired of wondering why I survived it all
I'm tired of wondering what the reasons
  of my survival were
I'm tired of wondering when my education will help me
I'm tired of wondering when my training
  will make me soar
I'm tired of wondering when I have to
  stop fighting for my life
I'm tired of people telling me to suck it
  up, I'm not the only one
I'm tired of hearing there are people worse off
I'm tired of being told to stop the self-pity
I'M TIRED OF IT ALL
I'm tired of showing a brave front
I'm tired of pretending I'm okay
I'm tired of rising above it
I'm tired of laughing but crying inside
I'm tired of struggling forward by dying inside
I'M TIRED

I just want comfort, laughter, lots of
        laughter, happiness, and love
Haven't I been through enough
I at least deserve that

Deception by Charm

I was deceived by the charm

A smile so sweet
Now a smile with evil undertone
The warmth of his touch
Now burns a branding of pain
Passionate kiss
Now venom poisoning, weakening

Eyes of an angel
Look of demon
Soothing heartbeat
Cold as ice
Lies, lies, all lies
Amazing facade
Deception well hidden

I was deceived by the charm

Unexpected Faces

In my need of strong support
I found some unexpected faces
I always had to be strong alone
You gave me more strength

My wonderful friendly faces
I was on the verge of extinction
You came to my side
Awaiting me with open arms

My beautiful faces
I had tears streaming
You helped me wipe them away
You didn't judge me

My kind, warm faces
I wanted to fight for my family
You didn't question
You said as long as you're happy

My unexpected faces
I know I deserve better
You agree I do
We know my heart will let go

My understanding faces
My heart leads the way
You allow me to be crazy
You allow me to be sad

My smiling faces
I want my family
You make me smile
You show me love

My friendly faces
I want my partner
You said give it time
You will hold my hand

My unexpected faces
I thank you for being there
You are my support
You are my family

Are You Here

Are you looking down
Do you see me
My eyes fill with tears
Needing one of our talks
Wanting to just get away
Are you here
I can't sense you
If I turn to my side
Will I see you
Longing for your hug
Your words, "All will be okay"
Please be here
Dry my tears
I miss you
My strength

I Respect You

You spoke your truth
You don't hide who you are
You don't care what others think
They don't understand
But they still love you
They still accept all of you
I remember the pain
I remember the silence
I'll never forget your cruel words
I respect your honesty
The one time I needed you
You opened the door
You listened
You handed the keys
You closed the door
Not a word was spoken
But your actions spoke volumes
I'll always hold dear that kindness
I'll always be grateful for that day
I respect your honesty
I may have been denied your love
No kisses, no hugs, no "I love you"
But that one gesture of kindness
Meant everything
Thank you

I Want to Hate You

I want to wish disaster befall you
So you struggle every day
But I don't hate you

I want a house to fall on you
To get rid of the evil
But I don't hate you

I want to wish you illness
So you can suffer
But I don't hate you

I want to wish you betrayal
So you feel the agony
But I don't hate you

I want to wish you harm
So you feel pain
But I don't hate you

I want to wish you solitude
So you feel the emptiness
But I don't hate you

I want to hate you
So I can be free
But I can't hate you

All I Need

Simple Pleasures
Is all I need
To be present
Share intimate details
Listen
Conversations about everything and nothing
Simple Pleasures
Is all I need
Honesty
Trust
Transparency
Laughter
Simple Pleasures
Is all I need
Priceless time together
Not money
Not materials
Life shared
Simple Pleasures
Is all I need

Ultimate Betrayal

No fight left
All came crashing down
Realizing those who never knew you
Have decided to end your life
Everything fades
Anger rises
Thoughts race
Where did I go wrong
Why must I fight
Two angels lend a hand
Hope arises
Trust has dwindled to a select few
Lost faith in anything
My angel brings courage
Inspires the fight
Subsides the anger
Hardens the heart
Cynicism at its max
Nothing like your flesh
Your ultimate love
A love to die for
Betrays you and all trust vanished
A soul so damaged has become cold
My angel, give me light
Is it enough

Escape

Light dimmed
Shadows call
Protect yourself
Guard yourself
Isolation

Solitude

No one can make me feel more
Pain
Isolation
Sadness
Than you

You

You are my love
My happiness
My solace
You are my pain
My sadness
My destruction

Déjà Vu

I had a dream
Filled with pride
It was stolen
I retreated to darkness
Filled with solitude
It was safe

You appear luminous
Filled with hope
It was bright
I walked toward light
Filled with faith
It was peace

A new dream emerged
Filled with love
It was warm
I smiled with tears
Filled with happiness
It was surreal

Déjà vu
Dream is stolen
Light has dimmed
Warmth dissipated
Smile hiding tears
Sadness—peace a memory

Words

Invisible
Solitude
Abandoned
Regardless what stage in life, those
        are ever-so-present words
The only constant
The only truth
Speak up
Express your emotions
Show your love
Regardless what stage in life, those
        are tormenting phrases
Best only in movies
Only in fantasy
Karma
Envisioning
Hard work
Regardless what stage in life, those are
        words of false pretense
Disheartening
Only devastation
Faith
Hope
Love
Regardless what stage in life, those words paralyze
Cause unrelenting pain
Ultimate demise

AriLu

As if in a dream
Endless road
No one around
Lost in thought
I see you
So vivid, so real
I can touch you
See your smile
Purity, innocence
Simply smiling
All I see is your precious faces
So peaceful, a blessing
Giving me faith
Hope
A warm breeze on a summer's night
Arms open soaring to the heavens
Freedom
Eternal peace
Sunset, the calm after the chaos
Bright orange, warm glow
All that is good, pure
That is you
Carefree
True bliss
My sweet piece of heaven
My sanity, my peace, my light
"My cup runneth over" (Psalm 23:5)

The Edge

Teetering on the edge
Hear the call
Swaying
No hand stretched
Feel the wind
Abandon your fears
Staggering close
No one is calling
Reel you in
Don't look down
Close your eyes
Nothing there
Find your peace

Empty heart
Empty soul

Extreme sadness
Extreme pain

Loneliness
Darkness

Invisible

Locked doors
Ignored calls
Unanswered texts
Radio silence
A ghost
Can't drop by
Can't call
Tired of texts
Darkness
Nowhere to be found
Abandoned
Alone
Sadness
Pain
Darkness, help me
Shelter me
Hide me
Protect me
Set me free
Demons subside
Smile through loneliness
Laugh behind tears
Hear my scream
Feel my pain
Shadows set me free

Not a Fairy Tale

No one shows up at your desperate time
No one dies for your honor
No one holds you close until all is okay
No one answers the phone when you're fighting tears
No one is there to save you
No one promises to always be there
No one shares your life
No one walks beside you
No one professes their love
No one fights for your love
No one is there
No one

Abandoned

Conceived by lust
Born unwanted
Unprotected
Innocence lost
Lived in fear
Lost faith
Always teetering on the edge
Constant struggle
Demons haunt
Light burns
No sincere smile
No pure laughter
Just existence

A Mistake

I was never your child
Brought into this world
Without love
Without passion
Another mistake
A burden
Innocence stolen
Never carefree
Always fighting for myself
Tring to not give up
Putting on a perfect show
Smiling for the camera
All the while screaming
Wondering when I'll be free
Time has passed
I'm still fighting
I'm still searching for peace
Happiness
Demons creep
Forever haunted
My broken heart
Always trying to heal
My soul always searching for light
Darkness will always reign
Tears will always flow
Sadness forever prominent
Heart never healed
As I lay in bed

Eyes slowly close
My heart aching
Sadness piercing
Wishing to never wake

Sliver

Broken bones
Shattered hope
Emotional damage
Fragmented heart
No love
No hugs
Scarred
Trying to mend
Closed eyes
Imagining better
Tears flow
Scars burn
Heart hurts
Mind racing
Trying, trying
Tears flowing
Can't breathe
Suffocating
Paralyzed
I'm trying
Step forward
Smile
Laugh
Can't stop
Tears flow
Heart stops
Everything still
Silence
Peace

My Extradition

You planted the seed
A deliberate LIE
Allowed the imagination soar
You stole my Heart
Literally broke it
Never once cared who got hurt
Damaged you caused
Your selfishness
Your callousness
EVIL
Not once did it occur to you
The devastation of your actions
You twisted the dagger
Upon my Heart's return
You banish me
Extradited
Terminate my existence
EVIL
My Heart will never forget
LOVE, JOY, CAREFREE LIFE
Heart will always cherish the happiness once felt
Heart will always remember
No matter how hard you try to erase me
Heart will always be one with the broken one
Your dark soul heartlessly caused

Nothing but Evil

You sit on your mighty high horse
Judging everyone
Inflicting pain
Using any means to destroy
Not giving a shit who you hurt
Sitting on your hypocritical moral throne
Playing the martyr role all too well
You believe your lies to be true
Not realizing you've been caught up
The only thing you care about is you
You don't know love
You don't know compassion
You don't know family
You hide behind "faith"
Those you've tried to destroy
And continue to destroy
Are stronger than you think
Are smarter than you give them credit
You think you're untouchable
You think you're loved
Some are there out of obligation
Some are trapped there
You will never know love
All you care about is destruction
You enjoy seeing others' pain
Especially misery by your malicious hand
You laugh at the tears you have caused
Evil is in all forms
You have the perfect disguise
Evil at its best

You Wish

You wish I would commit suicide
You could be the grieving mother
Oh, what a troubled soul she was
You milking every condolence
Every compassionate hug
All the while they not knowing
You are the root of the problem
You wish I would commit suicide
All secrets stay behind closed doors
All your lies will never be exposed
You'll only be seen as the grieving mother
You'll be smiling behind those crocodile tears
Denying you are the root of the pain
You wish I would commit suicide
Your problem is silenced
Your reputation unblemished
You revel in the attention
You smirk at your victory
You'll hide it well
You are the root of searing scars
You wish I would commit suicide

Discarded

You were supposed to be the parent I never had
You were supposed to wipe my tears
You were supposed to hold my hand
You were supposed to hug me tight
You were supposed to tell me all will be okay
But you stood by and allowed the cruelty to continue
Making you just as
Cold
Cunning
Manipulative
Deceitful
Heartless
You were supposed to be the parent I never had
You ended up abandoning the child you never wanted
Just like them

Nothing but a Burden

You can continue to tell yourself you love us
But we all know we were just a burden
Demons that haunt
Scars that burn
Forever reminders of a childhood lost
You can continue to convince yourself and your God
That you were there
We know the truth
You finally got what you wanted

You are the epitome of deceit,
        manipulation, and hypocrisy

Suicide or Fight

Fighting for life way too long
Frightened as a toddler
Trying to forget the nights of pure evil
Wondering will it ever end
The nightmares won't end
Years pass
Finally the last fight from this pure evil
Opened the door to a horrific betrayal
No light to guide the way
Always guarded
Time passes
An emptiness that will never be filled
A heart never to be whole
A sadness so profound
A pain so piercing
No one to lean on
No one to hold me close
No one to just be there
A few years of light and warmth
A betrayal like no other
Devastation
All trust lost
All dreams obliterated
Darkness overwhelms
Sadness
Solitude
Pain
Broken
Scarred
Just existing

I Need a Distraction

I need a distraction to forget
To numb me from my pain
Release my dark memories
Replace them with peace
Maybe even a little laughter
Heal my heart
Stop the tears
I need a distraction to forget
Set me free
Feel a warm hug
A tender kiss
Help me trust
Let me enjoy the little things
A child's carefreeness
A child's uncontrollable laughter
I need a distraction to forget
I want to enjoy Little One's sweet smile
My Baby running in the park
Kicking the ball around
Trying to play basketball
Reading a book
Creating art
I need a distraction to forget
My pain that never ends
My haunting that lingers
The light that burned
The nightmares
Show me peace
Release me
I need a distraction to forget

I Turn to My Side

I'm screaming inside
I turn to my side—no one is there
I'm crying
I turn to my side—no one is there
My pain is intense
I turn to my side—no one is there
Scars are piercing
I turn to my side—no one is there
Demons haunting
I turn to my side—no one is there
Laughter to hide all fear
I turn to my side—no one is there
Smile to camouflage sadness
I turn to my side—no one is there
Darkness consumes
I turn to my side—no one is there
Nowhere to run no escape
I turn to my side—no one is there
Infinite loneliness

Misleading

I thought I was healing
You by my side
I thought I was safe
False security
I thought I felt warmth
A constant shiver
I thought you a beautiful soul
Dimmed light
I thought you different
Truth destroyed all hope
Painful laughter
Saddened smile
Devastation
Destruction
Destroyed
Darkness

Disguised Evil

Not a movie
Not a fairy tale
No happy ending
No love
Darkness...Betrayal
Heartache...Emptiness
Sadness...Shattered
Rehearsed emotions
Empty words
Deceitful...Cold
Manipulating...Cunning
Evil in disguise

Continuous Darkness

You dimmed my light
It's nothing but a flicker
You were supposed to be different
You were supposed to restore my faith
Shattered
Too many pieces lost
You were supposed to be true
You were supposed to restore my trust
Nightmares rage
Darkness beckons
You were supposed to be pure happiness
You were supposed to be my warmth
Scars ignited, so fierce
Excruciating pain rekindled
You were supposed to be tender
You were supposed to release my fears
Holding back tears as I see you
Dying inside as you hold me
You were supposed to be faithful
You were supposed to be honest
Can't breathe
Heartbroken
You were supposed to be my peace
You were supposed to be my ultimate love
Destroyed. Devastated.
Betrayed. Used.
You were the evil I tried to escape
You were the ultimate agony

Devastation

I fell in love
You earned my trust
There it was in black and white
Your indiscretions
Given the chance for honesty
You lied without hesitation
My heart sank
My trust disappeared
I asked again
You lied again without blinking an eye
My pain sharpened
Devastation
No remorse
No empathy
Just like the others—selfish
My guard will always be up
My trust diminished
Damaged

Guard Down

I let my guard down
I let you in
I trusted you
You took advantage
You cut me deep
You disrespected me
I was happy
I felt safe
I thought it was love
You made me a fool
You lied
You destroyed me
How stupid was I
How blinded
How vulnerable
You never cared
You opened my eyes
You caused excruciating pain
Scars will never heal
Scars will always burn
Scars permanently tattooed
Because of you, all hope is lost
Because of you, love will always be an illusion
Because of you, faith is inconceivable

Meaningless

I embraced you
I let you in my life
We shared intimacies
We cried about our past
I trusted you
I loved you
You lied
Your words mean nothing
I thought you a light
I thought you different
You had your darkness
You're no better
If anything, you're worse
You took advantage of my past
You're like the rest
Hide behind religion
Perception of good
Pretend to be honest
Manipulated trust
The uttered words "I love you"
Hollow words
For a dark soul can have no warmth
Cold, calculated, callous

I Hate That I

I hate I cried tears for you
I hate I loved you
I hate I still want you
I hate I trusted you
I hate I let my guard down
For what
A smile
A hug
A kiss
A touch
Nothing but
False sense of security
Wounds forever burn
A heart to never heal
A void to never be filled
Solely existing but not living
Waiting for the day
My light to extinguish
For my pain to cease
To be set free

Let Me Go

This darkness weighs
My pain won't subside
My eyes won't stop tearing
Every breath aches
A lump in my throat
I remember the warmth
I remember the smile
The adventure
Now
All I feel is lost
Devastation
Shattered
Alone
The truth will set you free
Be honest, show me I can trust
Show me hope
Or just let me go
So I can try and pick up the pieces
I can close my eyes and sleep
Peace and darkness
Just stay closed

Crutch

You are the root of my sadness
My love for you is my crutch
I know you are my pain
My heart clouds my brain
I know you won't change
Your lies
Your indiscretions
Your selfishness
Hoping my love is enough
Deep down knowing it never will be
You provoke my cynicism
I wish for the "happily ever after"
The fantasy
I know life is unfair
I know people don't change
I know my love is not enough
I desire you to be truthful
I crave you to be faithful
I yearn for your unconditional love
You are the root of my sadness
You are my illness
You are my pain

Missing

I needed you
You ignored me
I was on the edge
You were nowhere
I needed you
You vanished
I was on the ledge
You were nowhere
I needed you
You disappeared
I was ready—jump
You were nowhere
I needed you
You dismissed
I was ready—forever sleep
You were nowhere

Torment

My sadness overwhelms
My tears stream uncontrollably
My heart aches intensely
I can't smile without sadness
I can't laugh without tears
I can't breathe without pain
I close my eyes to find happiness
I close my eyes to find peace
I close my eyes to find love
Nothing makes me smile truthfully
Nothing makes me laugh honestly
Nothing makes me love purely
All I have is sadness and pain

Convince Yourself

Your words are meaningless
Your smile cold
Your laugh cruel
Your touch insincere

Your words are lies
Your smile cunning
Your laughter evil
Your touch a notch

You say you're the nicest person
Are you trying to convince yourself
Actions speak different
They scream disrespect

You say you're a person of devout faith
Are you trying to convince yourself
Actions speak different
They yell betrayal

You say you're a person of truth
Are you trying to convince yourself
Actions speak different
They boast deceit

I showed you honesty
I showed you respect
I showed you pure love
I showed you trust

Now I'm on the edge
Waiting for the final shove
Accepting the cruelty that is you
Embracing the harsh truth

Allowing the darkness warmth in
Acknowledging there is no one true
Accepting it was all a lie
Welcoming the end and finding peace

Deceptive

You were my light
You made me smile
You made me laugh

You were my healing
Your gentle kiss
Your warmth

You were my peace
Your tight embrace
I felt safe

It was all a lie
Your betrayal
Your disrespect

Nothing was real
No meaning
No truth

It was all in vain
It was all pain
Sadness

I see you
My heartache intensifies
I can't breathe

I kiss you
I die inside
I wait for the end

You were never true
Lies
Deception

You were never love
Lust
Selfishness

You were never light
Coward
Hypocrite

Disrespected

You hide behind your faith
Claiming you are true
Announcing your goodness
Are you trying to convince yourself?

Does your faith condone deceit?
Does your faith tolerate betrayal?
Does your faith accept disrespect?
Do you just ask for forgiveness?

You hide behind your faith
All the while causing destruction
Pain. Sadness. Distrust. Darkness.
Are you proud?

I'm a nice person
Are you trying to convince yourself?

Constantly lying
Pretending to care
Being unfaithful
Disrespectful

Did it ever occur to you the…
Damage of your actions
Destruction of trust
Devastation of devotion

Do you even care?
Why should you
You took what you wanted
Another pawn for your collection

Selfish
Are you happy?

Darkness emerges

When

When will you realize we are meant to be
We share everything
Our darkest moments
Roaring laughter
Love of music
When will you open your eyes, we are meant to be
Spending endless nights
Talking, crying, laughing
Sharing everything
We are perfect
When
When I have left
When I found someone new
When my heart can't take the pain
When my happiness turns to sadness
When
When I walk away from my bestie
And we both are lost in darkness

Give Up, Stay, Disappear

My head says, Give up, you're an idiot
My heart says, Stick around, be close
My head yells, RUN
My heart says, Walk near

You're my addiction
My laughter
My sanity

Why can't you feel my love
Why can't you take the blinders off
Why do you continue to break me

I won't be here forever
My heart can only take so much
My sadness needs to end

I fear I'm damaged
I fear I will always be hurt
I fear I will never leave this prison

My inner struggle
Run, be free
Stay, keep fighting

Simply DISAPPEAR

My Addiction, My Destruction

My thoughts race
Fighting emotions
I need a fix
Your laughter
I call just to hear your voice
Slumped in my chair with a smile

Again I know I have to let you go

My pain screaming RUN
My tears burn like acid
Mind fighting my heart
I need a dose
Just a small one
I come over

I need to let go

I'm free enjoying the day
Days pass, I'm good
No, my heart jerks
All too familiar ache
I cave, I need a form of you
I bring up your picture

Saddened, I need to let you go

I write, draw, listen to music
Anything to distract me
You're in everything
Anything I do, I see you
I yell, cry, fight
I need you here

I need to let you go

My darling
My addiction
You have me
Defeated
Damaged
Destroyed

Jaded, Guarded, Fractured

I longed for your smile
I yearned your kisses
I craved to hold you
Lies
Betrayal
Mistrust
I wanted to believe you different
I wanted true happiness
I wanted the fantasy
Nothing but a cardboard cutout
Nothing but emotionless grin
Nothing but a shattered dream
I needed for us to be genuine
I needed for us to be honest
I needed for us to be love
Not deception
Not settlement
Not lust
I remain jaded
I remain guarded
I remain fractured
Because lying is so easy for you
Because cheating is just second nature for you
Because callousness is part of you
Gifts without meaning
Conversations without sincerity
All just a game
I remain jaded
I remain guarded
I remain fractured

Shit Show

You don't know me
But you judge me
We never had a conversation
But you judge me
You believe gossip
You judge me

You weren't in my life
But you judge me
You weren't there as I raised my children
But you judge me
You listen to those who think they know
But you judge me

Not once did you call
Not once did you visit
Not once did you ask me
You don't know me
You only judge me

You think you're better
You think I'm nothing
You show your hypocrisy
You don't know me
You judge me

Are you threatened by my independence
Are you jealous my children don't run from me
Are you afraid of my truth
You don't know me
You only feel entitled to judge me

We Just Dealt with It

We never even considered suicide
We never considered mass shooting
Those words weren't in our vocabulary
We dealt with it
It was what we were given
It was what we had to live with
We accepted our damage
We hoped for better
We may even have lost faith in everything
Lost faith in most everyone
Lost trust
Became cynical
We didn't kill innocence
Even if our innocence was taken
Had to grow up too fast
We didn't commit random acts of violence
Even if violence was bestowed us
We dealt with it
Therapy was only a vocabulary word
Coping mechanisms were only phrases
We suffered in silence
We moved forward holding back tears
We still walked tall as if nothing was wrong
"I love you" weren't words we heard
Hugs weren't a familiar concept
Our guard was always up
Smiles hiding pain
Depression just a word with no meaning

We just pushed forward
Waiting for the elusive unconditional love
Waiting for the happiness others experienced
We just dealt with it
A darkness never to subside
Faded light
Sad eyes
Waiting for the warmth of peace
Broken soul
Trying not to fall off the ledge
Just teetering
Irreparable damage
Hairline hope

Sad Eyes

With a heavy heart
I see the sunrise
A blurred orange light
Peering through cloudy skies
With a heavy heart
Sad eyes, I face days without you
A foggy day, wondering what you're doing
Are you missing me as much I do you
With a heavy heart
Tears flowing as I try to stop the pain
Missing your smile, your tight hugs
A laughter so contagious I smile through my tears
With a heavy heart
Tears in my eyes
Emptiness
I wait for your return home

Loneliest Alone

Just because there's a person around
Doesn't mean you're not alone
Just because you hear footsteps
Doesn't mean you're not alone
Just because you hear voices
Doesn't mean you're not alone

You're not spending time with the person
You're not walking with the person
You're not speaking with the person

Just existing
It's the loneliest alone
Not sharing your life

I Am Not Your Prison

I am not your prison
I will not be the reason you didn't reach your goals
I will not be your excuse
I am not your prison
You created your own obstacles
You are responsible for your choices
I am not your prison
I will not be your excuse
You want to hide behind a facade
You want to live the lie
I am not your prison
I will not be your excuse

You Don't See Me

You don't see me
You don't know me
The torment
The empty soul
You don't see me
You don't know me
Just judgment
Just persecution
You don't see me
You don't know me
My pain
My sorrow
You don't see me
You don't know me
Fabrications
Accusations
You don't see me
You don't know me
This hollow entity
This lasting sadness
You don't see me
You don't know me
Alienated
Discarded
You don't see me
You don't know me
Alone

Survival

I survive on memories of you
Your beautiful smile
Roaring laughter
My survival is all you
Running carefree
Everlasting tight hugs
My survival, thoughts of you
Sweet, "I love you"
Snuggling close
I'm here because of you
Until your hand is in mine again
My beautiful soul, Little One

About the Author

This Chicago native enjoys her time with her children and friends. Sandoval has been writing since she was in grammar school. She continues to write when inspiration strikes or when she needs to release what's flowing through her head. Growing up as an inner-city kid and in a tumultuous environment, Sandoval continues to use her writing as an outlet to heal.